DEVELOPING THE INNER MIND

By

Phillip Rich

EKKILISIA PROPHETIC APOSTOLIC MINISTRIES, INC.

Take note that the name satan is not capitalized. We choose not to acknowledge him, even to the point of violating grammatical rules.

Table of Contents

Thinking God's Thoughts

I want to talk about thinking the thoughts of God and developing your spiritual mind. I also want to show you how to have the thoughts of God flowing into your spiritual mind at all times. There is a natural mind for your natural body and a spiritual mind for your spiritual body. You are both natural and spiritual. You are not just a physical person living in a physical body. That is only half of the equation. Inside of you is a spirit man that Paul calls the inner man of the heart.

I want to release some of this to you so that you can have spiritual thoughts, thinking the thoughts that God thinks. Then God can also think through you. What can that mean? It means you can know things others won't know. You will know things that God knows. How many have heard of the revelation gifts: the word of knowledge, the word of wisdom and discerning of spirits. This teaching will allow you to operate in the revelation gifts at a level much higher than you have ever seen before. Do you have a thirst to be used by God more than you every have been before?

Matthew 5:6; "Blessed are they which do hunger and thirst after righteousness: for they shall be filled."

If you are not hungry and thirsty you won't be filled. I pray that you are hungry for this because I can't give you anything you are not hungry for. I cannot force anyone even if it is for their own good, but God can make you hungry, thirsty and cause you to desire the things He desires. When that desire comes, it is a tree of life (Prov. 13:12).

Mark 11:24; "Therefore I say unto you, What things soever ye desire, when ye pray, believe that ye receive them, and ye shall have them."

1

Proverbs 18:1; "Through desire a man, having separated himself, seeketh and intermeddleth with all wisdom."

Desire is hunger and thirst. We need to hunger and thirst after the things of God and after righteousness. Righteousness is intimacy with God.

For twenty years I have sought the Lord for this revelation. I would get little bits and pieces, but never the full revelation. Then, the Spirit of the Lord enabled me to pick up some revelation from a man of God. He talked about hearing God through flowing thoughts. When he said that, something went off on the inside of me and I began to study. I started seeing something I had never seen before. We have two minds, not just one, and I will prove it to you using scripture. It is all through the Word of God.

You can develop your spiritual mind to the point where you think what God thinks. When you look at somebody, you will think God's thoughts about them. How powerful prophetically can that be? You might be in prayer, praying about a situation and begin to think what God thinks about it. That will change everything.

In every chapter I will unveil something new, something fresh that will enlighten you and change your life. Many of you will begin to operate in a different realm of the spirit operating by the mind of Christ.

Isaiah 55:6; "Seek ye the LORD while he may be found, call ye upon him while he is near:"

The first thing for developing and coming into the thought realm of God is that you must seek Him with all your heart. Seek the Lord and begin to call upon Him. When we begin to seek Him He starts to release something to us.

Isaiah 55:7; "Let the wicked forsake <u>his way</u>, and the unrighteous man <u>his thoughts</u>: and let him return unto the LORD, and he will have mercy upon him; and to our God, for he will abundantly pardon."

This scripture is talking about man's own natural ways of doing things and his natural thoughts. Let the wicked and unrighteous forsake their natural way and natural thoughts. We are not supposed to live according to our natural thoughts and natural ways. Don't live your spiritual life according to the natural. It doesn't work.

Isaiah 55:8-9; "For my thoughts are not your thoughts, neither are your ways my ways, saith the LORD. For as the heavens are higher than the earth, so are my ways higher than your ways, and my thoughts than your thoughts."

I have heard this preached and it has been said that we can't think the thoughts of God because they are too high. We can't know His ways because they are beyond our knowing. That is not what this scripture is saying. In the verse before these, we are told to forsake our thoughts and our ways. Why say that? It is because we are supposed to pick up the thoughts of God and follow the ways of God. Otherwise, why forsake something? There are thoughts and ways that are greater.

Thoughts in the Hebrew means God's intentions, plans and purposes.

Do you believe that God wants us that have an understanding and knowing of His intentions, plans and purposes? How would you ever fulfill the will of God if you didn't know it? How are you going to ever please God if you don't know what pleases Him? How are you going to live for God if you don't know how to live for Him?

Ways means a course or mode of action. It is God's way of doing things, His nature. His ways are His mode of operation. It is how God operates. Moses knew the ways of God while the people only knew the works.

Psalms 103:7; "He made known his ways unto Moses, his acts unto the children of Israel."

Because Moses knew the ways of God he could operate in the signs and wonders of God. As soon as you know the ways of God, you will also operate in the power and glory of God as well in the fullness of His Spirit.

Isaiah 55:10-11; "For as the rain cometh down, and the snow from heaven, and returneth not thither, but watereth the earth, and maketh it bring forth and bud, that it may give seed to the sower, and bread to the eater: So shall my word be that goeth forth out of my mouth: it shall not return unto me void, but it shall accomplish that which I please, and it shall prosper in the thing whereto I sent it."

These verses tell us how to know His thoughts and His ways.

Rain is the water of life, of the spirit. We even sing songs that say let the river flow. Water in this verse refers to the flowing of the Holy Spirit.

Let's go to the book of Joel to look at something.

Joel 2:12-15; "Therefore also now, saith the LORD, turn ye even to me with all your heart, and with fasting, and with weeping, and with mourning: And rend your heart, and not your garments, and turn unto the LORD your God: for he is gracious and merciful, slow to anger, and of great kindness, and repenteth him of the evil. Who knoweth if he will return and repent, and leave a blessing behind him; even a meat offering and a drink offering unto the LORD your God? Blow the trumpet in Zion, sanctify a fast, call a solemn assembly:"

It's time to gather the people together. It's time to call the people to prayer.

Joel 2:16; "Gather the people, sanctify the congregation, assemble the elders, gather the children, and those that suck the breasts: let the bridegroom go forth of his chamber, and the bride out of her closet."

Everybody should come and pray. There is no excuse for not praying as a church according to this scripture.

4

Joel 2:17; "Let the priests, the ministers of the LORD, weep between the porch and the altar, and let them say, Spare thy people, O LORD, and give not thine heritage to reproach, that the heathen should rule over them: wherefore should they say among the people, Where is their God?"

Even the ministers should be on their faces praying and seeking the face of God. Weeping is birthing the next move of God. What is going to happen when we do all of that?

Joel 2:28; "And it shall come to pass afterward [after the praying and fasting], **that I will pour out** [like water] **my spirit upon all flesh; and your sons and your daughters shall prophesy, your old men shall dream dreams, your young men shall see visions:"**

Are you ready for your sons and daughters to start prophesying? Are you ready for old men to dream dreams and young men to have some visions? Are you ready for dreams, visions, revelations and the supernatural power of God being poured out?

Joel 2:29; "And also upon the servants and upon the handmaids in those days will I pour out my spirit."

The servants and handmaids are those who desire to be used by God.

Joel 2:30; "And I will shew wonders in the heavens and in the earth, blood, and fire, and pillars of smoke."

These are signs, wonders and miracles that will shake nations with the gospel of Jesus.

Can you see how awesome this is and what God is saying to us? How can we know His thoughts? We need to seek Him for the outpouring of His Spirit upon us. God said, "*If My people who are called my My name…*" not if the world will pray or the nation repent. We can't expect a nation to repent when many do not know Jesus as Lord and Savior.

Isaiah 55:10; "For as the rain cometh down, and the snow from heaven, and returneth not thither, but watereth the earth, and maketh it bring forth and bud, that it may give seed to the sower, and bread to the eater:"

Do you want the water of God to be poured out on all flesh? Do you realize that all flesh didn't have an outpouring on the day of Pentecost? Three thousand did and later it was five thousand. We see pockets of people having a great outpouring, but it has not yet hit all flesh. I believe we can pray, seek God and it will happen for us as well.

Isaiah 55:11; "So shall my word be that goeth forth out of my mouth: it shall not return unto me void, but it shall accomplish that which I please, and it shall prosper in the thing whereto I sent it."

Word in this verse is the Hebrew word *dabar* (*daw-baw'*). This is the same as the word rhema that we see in the New Testament. Rhemas are the word that has come alive by the Holy Spirit. It is the living word, a now word as if God said it for the very first time.

God wants us to fill our minds and hearts with the dabar of God. People who pray hear God. People who don't pray, don't hear. The level of your prayer is the level of your hearing. Pray a little bit, hear a little bit. Pray more and you hear more. Intercessors are going to hear God. When you are focusing on God, talking to God and are in His presence, He is going to speak to you and you will hear Him. His Word will come alive to you as you read, study and meditate on it. You will get the debars of God.

Isaiah 55:12; "For ye shall go out with joy, and be led forth with peace: the mountains and the hills shall break forth before you into singing, and all the trees of the field shall clap their hands."

Why are you going out with joy and being led forth with peace? It is because now you are having an outpouring of the Spirit upon your life through fasting, prayer and time in His Word. You are hearing God and getting His thoughts. The most powerful way God speaks to us is with flowing thoughts that come to your spiritual mind. You begin to have His thoughts and know His ways.

Have you ever known something and didn't know how you knew it? You just knew. What happened? The thoughts of God were made known to you.

When I ask people how they hear God's voice, some will tell me they hear a booming voice. If you are a child of God, He is not going to be booming His voice to you because He lives on the inside of you. 1 Corinthians chapters 3 and 6 both tell us that the Spirit of God dwells in us. If the Spirit of God dwells in you, where is He going to speak? It will be in you to your spiritual mind.

Your natural mind is connected to your natural body so that body can operate. Inside of you is a spiritual man that has a spiritual mind. All that is needed is to get that mind renewed. Then the mind of the Spirit will connect to your spiritual mind and you will begin to think His thoughts. You will know things that you can't know.

Going back to our scripture, you will be led because you will know what to do. You will have peace and joy because you are going to be doing exactly what you should be doing. Then because you know His thoughts and His ways, read what happens.

Isaiah 55:13; "Instead of the thorn shall come up the fir tree, and instead of the brier shall come up the myrtle tree: and it shall be to the LORD for a name, for an everlasting sign that shall not be cut off."

When Adam and Eve sinned, God told them the ground would be cursed and thorns would come up.[1] Isaiah 55:13 says that instead of the thorn, a fir tree would come up.

---

[1] Genesis 3:17-18

7

Isaiah 60:13; "The glory of Lebanon shall come unto thee, <u>the fir tree</u>, the pine tree, and the box together, to beautify the place of my sanctuary; and I will make the place of my feet glorious."

This speaks about the glory that will be upon us so that we are not toiling. Did you know that glory will cause wealth to be attracted to you? Read Isaiah 60:1-11. It says that because God has glorified us, the wealth of the Gentiles shall be brought to us.

You are working for it but not toiling. There is a difference between working and toiling. Toiling is holding down three jobs to make ends meet. It tears your body down and leaves you stressed out. Toiling is part of the curse.

If you know His thoughts and His ways then instead of thorns you will have the fir tree. You will be glorified. God's glory will come upon you and finances will be attracted to you as if you are a mighty magnet. Are you ready for the fir tree? That is what happens when you know His thoughts and His ways.

The brier represents hardship. Have you been through some hardships in your life where you lost a house, a vehicle, finances or something was stripped from you? Instead of the brier shall come up the myrtle, which represents prosperity. You will start being prosperous and blessed. It is all tied to the fact that now you are thinking His thoughts and know His ways.

That is the difference between having nothing and being blessed, suffering lack and having abundance, God using you in a powerful way and being in total darkness not understanding what you should do with your life. <u>Too many Christians are floundering when they should be flourishing.</u> Floundering is moving a lot and not getting anywhere.

Do you want to do actions that bring results, work a little and get a lot? You should be able to work less and get more. If the blessing is upon you and you know His thoughts and ways, you will.

I know one man who is making money in the stock market because he knows the thoughts and ways of God. God lets him know which stocks to buy and when to sell.

If you have been struggling to pay your bills, this may be hard for you to grasp. I know because I have been there myself. What caused me to come out of that was looking at the plan of God and how He thinks about my life and my purpose. I began to focus on my purpose in life instead of finances to fulfill something. I quit thinking about money and began to think about purpose. In other words, I started thinking God's thoughts. I found out what God wanted me to do and didn't base it on whether I could really afford it. When I think, *"Can I afford it?"* that is not the thoughts of God. It is a thought of the world or of satan.

Some of you need to get the words "can't afford" out of your vocabulary and you will prosper. Fast the word "can't" and read Philippians 4:13.

Philippians 4:13; "I can do all things through Christ which strengtheneth me."

Many years ago my parents moved us from the city to a farm. We had broiler houses of chickens that we raised for nine weeks. Then they were picked up and another batch of thousands of chicks were delivered for us to raise for nine weeks. We boys also had to bale and haul hay, split and stack wood. These were things I had never done in my life and so had no real understanding of what I was doing. We were constantly saying, *"We can't do this. We don't know how."* My dad lined us up and said, *"Boys, there is one word we are never going to use. If you say it, I will correct you severely for it. We will never use the word can't. If you don't know how to do something, then ask. If you still don't know how to do it, try something. I would rather have you try and not be able to do it than never have tried because you said you couldn't."* We found out we could and starting telling our dad that we could do it.

We need to get rid of the word can't. Instead, we need to say that "through Christ we can do all things". We can think His thoughts and know His ways. We can develop our spiritual mind. Trust in the Lord with all your heart and lean not to your own understanding. In all your ways acknowledge Him and He will direct your path.[2] Don't go with your natural mind but with your spiritual mind.

I am going to show you that your spirit has a mind. There are many scriptures in the Word of God about the mind of your spirit and how to develop it so that the mind of Christ will be yours. You will think what He thinks and know what He knows about things. How valuable could that be in everyday life? How many times do we not know what to do? If we had the mind of Christ, were developed in our spiritual mind we would know what He knows about it and would know what to do.

What about words of knowledge, wisdom and discerning of spirits? Can you imagine ministering to somebody and knowing what God knows about them? That means I would know the prayers they have been praying. Why would God tell me? It is because He wants them to know He knew what they had been praying.

1 John 5:14-15; "And this is the confidence that we have in him, that, if we ask any thing according to his will, he heareth us: And if we know that he hear us, whatsoever we ask, we know that we have the petitions that we desired of him."

In other words, if He has heard us that prayer is answered. So if God tells me what somebody has been praying for, then they know it is an answered prayer.

God doesn't hear all prayers and therefore doesn't answer all prayers. A prayer in fear, doubt and unbelief is not heard by God and therefore it is not answered. A prayer that is against God's Word, He doesn't hear and does not answer. Thank God He doesn't. Can you think back to some stupid prayers you have prayed and thank God He didn't answer them? We would have been in trouble if He had.

---

[2] Proverbs 3

Developing the Mind of Christ

We are supposed to be thinking the thoughts of God and knowing His ways. How do we do that? It is with our spiritual mind.

I believe what I am teaching is a key to the revelation gifts, and to developing the mind of Christ where you will literally think with the mind of Christ and be able to speak as an oracle of God. You will get detailed words of knowledge because you will know things you cannot otherwise know. In other words, you will know what God knows about a person, place or thing. You will know what to do in certain situations in your life when you don't know what to do. Your inner mind, the mind of your spirit, connected to the spiritual mind of God will begin to know what God knows.

The word of knowledge means the word of knowing something you cannot know. You don't receive that with your natural mind.

I want to prove to you there is a natural mind and a spiritual mind. They are not the same and will never be the same. For years I was taught that the natural mind would be renewed by the Word and would become a spiritual mind. That is not true and is not what the Bible teaches. The part of you that has to be renewed is the mind of your spirit.

I was taught this by the Spirit of God, though God used other people to unleash some scriptures that brought me to this revelation. You are two beings wrapped up in one. In fact your spiritual man has a mind just as your natural man has a mind. Your body has a soul, which is the natural thinking part of your body. I want to show you why your natural man has to have a mind and why your spirit man also has to have one. They both need minds to operate.

1 Corinthians 15:44; "It is sown a natural body; it is raised a spiritual body. There is a natural body, and there is a spiritual body."

Your spiritual body is more real than your flesh is. It is going to live forever. Your flesh will go back to the dust of the earth. The real you is not the outward part of you but the inward part.

1 Corinthians 15:46; "Howbeit that was not first which is spiritual, but that which is natural; and afterward that which is spiritual."

Again we read that there is the natural and the spiritual. God first formed the lump of clay. Then He breathed into the lump of clay and put His Spirit into it. I want you to see that the natural body was made first. We were first natural and then spiritual.

It is very important that you understand that there are two basic parts of you. You will never go farther in understanding the mind of Christ and your spiritual mind until you do. Once you understand your spiritual mind you will begin to concentrate on thinking the thoughts of God, listening to His thoughts and following His ways.

Ephesians 3:14-16; "For this cause I bow my knees unto the Father of our Lord Jesus Christ, Of whom the whole family in heaven and earth is named, That he would grant you, according to the riches of his glory, to be strengthened with might by his Spirit <ins>in the inner man</ins>;"

We all know about the outer man. We see ourselves and others who are around us. Paul is talking about the inner man in these verses.

2 Corinthians 4:16; "For which cause we faint not; but though our outward [physical] man perish, yet the inward man is renewed day by day."

Many of us recognize that every day we get a little older. Did you ever notice that the older you get the quicker the years go? I remember my grandpa, when he was in his 90's, saying he didn't know where the years had gone. He would look in the mirror, see an old man staring back at him and wonder who that man was. On the inside he felt like he was still in his 20's. My grandpa was looking at the outer man.

Look at what verse 16 says. **"The outward man perish, but the inward man is renewed day by day".** So when we renew our mind which mind is it talking about? The inward or the outward?

Romans 12:1-2; "I beseech you therefore, brethren, by the mercies of God, that ye present your bodies a living sacrifice, holy, acceptable unto God, which is your reasonable service. And be not conformed to this world: but be ye transformed by the renewing of your mind, that ye may prove what is that good, and acceptable, and perfect, will of God."

Which mind is being renewed? It is the spiritual mind because your natural mind can't be renewed to spiritual things. The natural mind is at enmity against God. How can you renew something that can't accept it? Your natural mind can't think spiritual thoughts. It can only think natural thoughts. But your spiritual mind can be renewed to the revelation of God. When you start operating heavily in the spiritual mind with the mind of Christ you will find that is where the power of God is. That is where signs, wonders and miracles, detailed prophesy, detailed words of knowledge and hearing the voice of God come from.

Romans 8:5-6; "For they that are after the flesh do mind the things of the flesh; but they that are after the Spirit the things of the Spirit. For to be carnally minded is death; but to be spiritually minded is life and peace."

Do you see the difference between the natural carnal mind and the spiritual mind?

I want to help you understand about the natural mind and the spiritual mind connected with the natural body and the spiritual body. If you think about it, your natural body needs a mind to operate in the natural. How could you make decisions, reason things out or do what you do in the natural without a natural mind. You wouldn't be able to. Your spiritual man needs a spiritual mind to be able to operate in the spirit.

We are supposed to operate in two realms all the time. We have dual citizenship. Your body enables you to be a citizen of the earth. Your spirit man enables you to be a citizen of heaven.

Romans 7:18; "For I know that in me (that is, in my flesh,) dwelleth no good thing: for to will is present with me; but how to perform that which is good I find not."

This verse is talking about operating only by the natural. The natural man will not always to what it should do. If you follow the appetites of the natural, you will do things you shouldn't do. If you live according to the flesh, you are going to sin.

Romans 7:19-20; "For the good that I would I do not: but the evil which I would not, that I do. Now if I do that I would not, it is no more I that do it, but sin that dwelleth in me."

Paul is talking about the natural man. He is saying he enters into sin and is sinning because he is living totally by the natural man.

Romans 7:21-22; "I find then a law, that, when I would do good, evil is present with me. For I delight in the law of God after the inward man:"

Even if I try to do good in the natural, I can't. Without God's help I can't keep from sinning. We have the sin nature until we accept Jesus Christ as Lord and Savior.

Verses 18-21 talked about your natural man. Verse 22 starts the verses which speak about the inward man, the natural mind and the spiritual mind.

Romans 7:23-25; "But I discern in my bodily members – in the sensitive appetites and wills of the flesh – a different law (rule of action) at war against the law of my mind (my reason) and making me a prisoner to the law of sin that swells in my bodily organs – in the sensitive appetites and wills of the flesh. O unhappy *and* pitiable *and* wretched man that I am! Who will release *and* deliver me from {the

14

shackles of} this body of death? Oh thank God! – He will! through Jesus Christ, the Anointed One, our Lord! So then indeed I of myself with the <u>mind and heart</u> serve the Law of God, but with the flesh the law of sin." [Amplified Bible]

Paul begins by talking about the natural mind. Reason is how your natural mind works. Your spiritual mind works by using the wisdom and knowledge of God. With the spiritual mind you are able to conquer your flesh and live a life above the bondages of this wretched and sinful world.

Are you ready to go beyond the limitations of this world, soaring into the spirit realm, thinking with the mind of Christ, speaking as an oracle of God, not limited by the natural limitations of this world and being able to know the thoughts and ways of God? This is what God has for each one of us and it is what He wants us to have. He wants us to go to another level in Him.

True meditation and contemplation is not done in the natural mind. It is done in the spirit. Words of knowledge, words of wisdom, discerning of spirits are received in your spiritual mind. The gifts of revelation are received from the mind of the Spirit being connected to your spiritual mind.

The Two Minds

We are going to be looking at how the natural mind and the spiritual mind work. We will also look at the differences and contrast the two. Then I will tell you **five things** that your spiritual mind can do that are different from your natural mind.

Romans 8:5-6; "For they that are after the flesh do mind the things of the flesh; but they that are after the Spirit the things of the Spirit. For to be carnally minded is death; but to be spiritually minded is life and peace."

Your natural mind thinks of natural things. Your spiritual mind thinks of spiritual things.

Romans 8:7; "Because the carnal mind is enmity against God: for it is not subject to the law of God, neither indeed can be."

Your natural mind can never become a spiritual mind. You can't renew your natural mind because it can never change. The natural mind works off of thoughts, reason, memorization, natural understanding and negative or positive response. It works off of natural things having to do with the natural stuff that enable you to operate in the natural.

Carnal in this verse means your natural way of thinking. Your natural mind cannot be spiritual. All your natural mind can do are the natural things because it is natural. Natural can't become supernatural. Your spirit is supernatural and the mind of your spirit has to be renewed and transformed by the Word of God.

Your natural mind cannot be transformed. It can only do what it does like a computer. Is your computer spiritual? Look at what you can do with it. You can type in information, store information, calculate numbers

16

and it can remember. Your computer is much like the natural mind. Your computer will never become spiritual any more than your natural mind will become spiritual. Your natural mind needs to do what it does so that you can operate in the natural.

We operate in two realms. Our natural mind allows us to operate in the natural with our natural body. Our spiritual man has a spiritual mind that enables the spiritual man to operate in the spirit realm.

Colossians 2:18; "Let no man beguile you of your reward in a voluntary humility and worshipping of angels, intruding into those things which he hath not seen, <u>vainly puffed up by his fleshly</u> [natural] <u>mind</u>,"

The natural mind can get puffed up and prideful.

Ephesians 2:2-3; "Wherein in time past ye walked according to the course of this world, according to the prince of the power of the air, the spirit that now worketh in the children of disobedience: Among whom also we all had our conversation in times past in the lusts of our flesh, fulfilling the desires of the flesh and of the mind; and were by nature the children of wrath, even as others."

Do you see what we are saying about the natural mind?

Romans 7:23; "But I discern in my bodily members – in the sensitive appetites and wills of the flesh – a different law (rule of action) at war against the law of my mind (my reason) and making me a prisoner to the law of sin that dwells in my bodily organs – in the sensitive appetites and will of the flesh." [Amplified Bible]

Romans 7:25; "O thank God! – He will! Through Jesus Christ, the Anointed One, our Lord! So then indeed I of myself with the mind and heart serve the Law of God, but with the flesh the law of sin." [Amplified Bible]

Verse 23 talks about the natural mind being reason. Verse 25 speaks about the spiritual mind that goes after the law of God. You cannot serve the law of God with your fleshly mind. Verse 25 connects mind and heart together and tells us that our heart (our inner man) has a mind. With that you serve the law of God.

This is important and you must see the difference between the natural mind and the spiritual mind before we go any further. This will make all the difference when we begin talking about the revelation gifts: words of knowledge, words of wisdom and discerning of spirits. You will find out how you receive these revelation gifts. Your spiritual mind can know things your natural mind doesn't know. You will begin ministering to people about things you don't know. You will know what to do when you normally wouldn't know what to do. And you will know what is coming when you wouldn't naturally know what is coming. This sounds like success and like the supernatural.

Let's look at the spiritual mind, the mind of the human spirit.

Hebrews 4:12; "For the word of God is quick, and powerful, and sharper than any twoedged sword, piercing even to the dividing asunder of soul and spirit, and of the joints and marrow, and is a discerner of the <u>thoughts and intents of the heart</u>."

I read here that your heart can think. If your spirit man can think, then your spirit man has a mind.

Proverbs 23:7; "For as he <u>thinketh in his heart</u>, so is he: Eat and drink, saith he to thee; but his heart is not with thee."

The heart is synonymous with the spirit or the inner man. We are not referring to the organ of your body that pumps blood. As a man thinketh in his heart must mean his heart thinks. If his heart thinks, then it has a mind. Your spirit man has a mind and can think.

Daniel 2:30; "But as for me, this secret is not revealed to me for any wisdom that I have more than any living, but for their sakes that shall make known the interpretation to the king, and <u>that thou mightest know the thoughts of thy heart</u>."

This is what Daniel said to the king because he was having a hard time knowing the thoughts of his heart.

If you have a hard time tapping into the mind of your spirit you may have a lot of dreams. I believe that dreams are a part of what we should be having. If you never hear God in the day it means you don't yet know how your spirit man thinks and picks up revelation. You are so busy you are blocking Him and not listening. So, God enables you to have a lot of dreams. He loves you so much He doesn't want you to miss the thoughts of your spirit that are connected to Him.

Where does the Spirit of God dwell? He dwells in our spirit. Spirit inhabits spirit. God wants to talk to us, but we need to learn how to listen and pick up spiritual thoughts. I call them flowing thoughts that do not come from your head. Yes, they still have to be judged by the Word of God.

1 Corinthians 2:9; "But as it is written, Eye hath not seen, nor ear heard, neither have entered into the heart of man, the things which God hath prepared for them that love him."

Let me say here, that, this verse is not talking about heaven. It is speaking about the things God has already prepared for us that He wants us to know about so that we can avail ourselves of the blessing.

1 Corinthians 2:10; "But God hath revealed them unto us by his Spirit: for the Spirit searcheth all things, yea, the deep things of God."

Can you see that there are things we need to know and don't yet know? But the Holy Spirit knows about all the provision that we need and will reveal them to our spirit. How does He do it? It is with flowing thoughts, knowings and revelations into the spirit realm.

1 Corinthians 2:11-12; "For what man knoweth the things of a man, save the spirit of man which is in him? even so the things of God knoweth no man, but the Spirit of God. Now we have received, not the spirit of the world, but the spirit which is of God; that we might know the things that are freely given to us of God."

19

Know, in verse 12, means thoughts. We have received the Spirit of God so that we might know. What part of us is going to know? It is our spiritual mind, the heart of man.

1 Corinthians 2:13; "Which things also we speak, not in the words which man's wisdom teacheth, but which the Holy Ghost teacheth; comparing spiritual things with spiritual."

The words man's wisdom teaches are the words we learned from birth, our natural language.

What is the language that the Holy Spirit gives us? It is the language of tongues, the prayer language. The more you pray in tongues the more your spiritual mind will know something.

1 Corinthians 2:14; "But the natural man receiveth not the things of the Spirit of God: for they are foolishness unto him: neither can he know them, because they are spiritually discerned."

Know in the Greek is *ginosko (ghin-oce'-ko)* meaning to have revelation knowledge of. The natural mind cannot operate in revelation knowledge, but your spirit man can because it has a mind that is capable of handling it. Your natural mind can only handle reason. Your spiritual mind can handle revelation. I believe reading this verse in the Amplified Bible will make it easier to understand.

1 Corinthians 2:14; "But the natural, nonspiritual man does not accept *or* welcome *or* admit into his heart the gifts *and* teachings *and* revelations of the Spirit of God, for they are folly (meaningless nonsense) to him; and he is incapable of knowing them – of progressively recognizing, understanding and becoming better acquainted with them – because they are spiritually discerned *and* estimated *and* appreciated." [Amplified Bible]

1 Corinthians 2:16; "For who hath known the mind of the Lord, that he may instruct [receive instruction from] him? But we have the mind of Christ."

The mind of the Lord is spiritual. He doesn't have a physical body and so doesn't have a natural mind like we do. You cannot know the mind of the Lord unless you have a spiritual mind to know His mind. We have the mind of Christ because we have a spiritual mind. We have to develop our spiritual mind, develop what He has given us.

I want to show you in scripture that you have to be renewed in the spirit of your mind.

Ephesians 4:17-23; "This I say therefore, and testify in the Lord, that ye henceforth walk not as other Gentiles walk, in the vanity of their mind, Having the understanding darkened, being alienated from the life of God through the ignorance that is in them, because of the blindness of their heart: Who being past feeling have given themselves over unto lasciviousness, to work all uncleanness with greediness. But ye have not so learned Christ; If so be that ye have heard him, and have been taught by him, as the truth is in Jesus: That ye put off concerning the former conversation [the former life style] **the old man, which is corrupt according to the deceitful lusts; And <u>be renewed in the spirit of your mind</u>;"**

Your natural mind cannot be renewed. It doesn't know what renewed is. Like a computer, it only knows the information that is fed into it. The real you is what is on the inside of you.

Five Things That Your Spiritual Mind Can Do

First and foremost is revelation. The natural man cannot receive the things of God because they have to be revealed to your spirit. Read 1 Corinthians 2:9-14. Your natural mind cannot operate in revelation. It can store facts and figures and memorize scripture.

The second thing is that your spiritual mind has a conscience. Your natural mind does not.

Even people who are lost still have a spirit and so will still have a conscience. You can sear it as with a hot iron and wind up with a reprobate mind. A reprobate mind is a spiritual mind that is void of conscience. That is dangerous. These people have no remorse about hurting or harming others.

Romans 8:16; "The Spirit itself [Himself] beareth witness with our spirit, that we are the children of God:"

The Spirit does not bear witness with my natural mind or my body. He bears witness with my spirit. Bear witness means to let my spirit know something. To witness is to tell something, to give information.

Romans 9:1; "I say the truth in Christ, I lie not, my conscience also bearing me witness in the Holy Ghost,"

Your conscience is part of your spiritual mind. Those who have studied the natural mind really don't know what to do with the conscience because it doesn't function with the natural mind. It only functions with the spiritual mind.

Why is conscience so important? The conscience is what lets you know right from wrong. It will let you know what you should or shouldn't be doing. Your conscience is the voice of your spirit to your natural mind. It conveys the information to your natural mind.

Here is the third thing that shows a difference between your spiritual mind and your natural mind.

1 Kings 10:24; "And all the earth sought to Solomon, to hear his wisdom, which God had put in his heart."

So, the third thing is wisdom. And it is not of the natural mind.

Your natural mind can figure out things based on something you did one time. You picked up a hot skillet with your hand instead of using something to insulate it and your hand hurt. Now your mind knows you must use a pot holder or glove. That is not wisdom, but natural deduction based on experience. Wisdom doesn't have to have an experience of anything. Wisdom comes from God. You will know what to do in a situation you have never been in before and have no experience to base it on. Your natural mind cannot do that. Your natural mind has to have an experience to bring deduction into play. Your spirit man only needs to hear wisdom from the spiritual mind of God.

The fourth thing is understanding.

Psalms 49:3; "My mouth shall speak of wisdom; and the meditation of my heart shall be of understanding."

Understanding doesn't come by the natural mind. It comes by the spiritual mind. Understanding means you know how it is going to work. You know doing one thing will bring something else. Another way of putting it is that you put two and two together and come up with the correct answer. Understanding does not come because of past experience though. It is because of revelation thoughts that come from the mind of the Spirit of God into your spiritual mind.

The imagination does not come from the natural mind. The imagination is the creative part of God imparted to the spirit of man.

1 Chronicles 29:18; "O LORD God of Abraham, Isaac, and of Israel, our fathers, keep this forever in the imagination of the thoughts of the heart of thy people, and prepare their heart unto thee:"

Are you aware that our cell phones came from imagination? So did airplanes, cars, clothes washers and dryers. Creative things don't come from the natural mind. They come from the inner mind, the mind of our spirit.

Even the unregenerate man who is lost without God still has a spiritual mind. To be dead spiritually doesn't mean you are nonexistent. That person's spirit still functions.

Psalms 19:14; "Let the words of my mouth, and the meditation of my heart, be acceptable in thy sight, O LORD, my strength, and my redeemer."

Do you know what the word meditation means? Look it up in the Hebrew. One of the renderings is imagination. To meditate means to imagine.

We are told all through the Word of God that we are supposed to be meditating in the Word. Did you know you are supposed to be imagining it working in your life?

By His stripes we are healed. Imagine yourself being healed because of the stripes of Jesus. Prosper and be in health as your soul prospers. Imagine yourself prospering. You have been sowing your seed and God is causing a harvest to come. Imagine it happening. That is the meditation of the Word. Your spirit man has the ability to do this.

"I didn't know I was supposed to use my imagination." You are.

Would you like to be able to see in the spirit very accurately? Work on your spiritual imagination by meditating on the Word and imagining the Word working. When you do that you are developing your ability to see accurately in the spirit.

Number five is impartation of knowledge about persons, places and things that you know nothing about. Only your spiritual mind can receive it. Your natural mind can never receive words of knowledge, words of wisdom or discerning of spirits.

1 Corinthians 12:4-8; "Now there are diversities of gifts, but the same Spirit. And there are differences of administrations, but the same Lord. And there are diversities of operations, but it is the same God which worketh all in all. But the manifestation of the Spirit is given to every man to profit withal. For to one is given by the Spirit the word of wisdom; to another the word of knowledge by the same Spirit;"

Who is giving these gifts? It is given by the Spirit of God.

The word of knowledge is knowing something you cannot know, but it is given to your spiritual mind. Your natural mind only handles natural knowledge that it knows or somebody tells it. The revelation gifts are connected directly to the spiritual mind.

Our Natural and Spiritual Senses

We have been making you aware that you have an outer man and an inner man according to scripture. Your outer man perishes and your inner man is renewed day by day. I thought we only had a natural mind and that somehow we were supposed to transform into a spiritual mind by scripture. What I didn't realize when I was studying is that there is a mind of your heart as well. You have a natural mind for your natural body and a spiritual mind for your spiritual body.

There were a lot of scriptures that I didn't understand until I saw we have a spiritual mind, an inner mind. In this chapter I want to talk about the natural mind and it's five senses as well as your spiritual mind and it's five senses.

With your natural body and your natural mind you contact the natural realm. With your spirit man and your spiritual mind you contact the realm of the spirit. That is how we operate in the spirit realm. If you had a natural body without a mind you wouldn't be able to operate in this world. Someone who is a vegetable in their mind is not able to get around. They would just be a flesh body and probably in the hospital.

Many don't understand that your natural mind enables you to operate in the natural. Your mind actually operates your five physical senses: seeing, hearing, touching, tasting and smelling. I researched the mind and the five senses on my computer and it explained that our five senses are sensory receptors. That means they gather information, put it into electrical impulses and sent it to the brain. The back part of your brain is specific to sight. Your eyes take in the image and sent it to the brain. Your skin is the sensory receptor for feeling heat, cold, pressure and so on. Each sense organ sends the information to a specific part of your brain and your brain decides what you are seeing, smelling, hearing, tasting and touching. If you didn't have a brain, it wouldn't do any good to have sensory receptors. You wouldn't be able to see, taste or hear without your brain.

The Bible speaks about five spiritual senses. If you don't have a spiritual brain, how will they work? They won't.

Isaiah 55:7-10; "Let the wicked forsake his way, and the unrighteous man his thoughts: and let him return unto the LORD, and he will have mercy upon him; and to our God, for he will abundantly pardon. For my thoughts are not your thoughts, neither are your ways my ways, saith the LORD. For as the heavens are higher than the earth, so are my ways higher than your ways, and my thoughts than your thoughts. For as the rain cometh down, and the snow from heaven, and returneth not thither, but watereth the earth, and maketh it bring forth and bud, that it may give seed to the sower, and bread to the eater:"

In this passage we just read God is telling us His thoughts are above our thoughts and His ways are above our ways. God wants us to think His thoughts, to know His ways.

1 Corinthians 2:14; "But the natural man receiveth not the things of the Spirit of God: for they are foolishness unto him: neither can he know them, because they are spiritually discerned."

So you have to have a spiritual mind to receive spiritual information. Your natural mind helps you operate in the natural. It can handle information you give it as well as experiences you have. It can operate your ability reason and memorize. You already saw it helps with your five natural senses. It is limited to the natural world.

If we are going to be spiritually minded we have to operate by another mind that can handle the conscience, imagination, intuition, revelation, understanding, words of knowledge and wisdom. Your natural mind cannot receive those things. Spiritual things are spiritually discerned, understood and received.

We are going to go through the five spiritual senses and I want to show you how your mind is able to process the information that your spiritual receptors give it by impulse. We have to learn to develop our

27

spiritual mind. Scripture tells us to be renewed in the spirit of our mind.[3] How do you renew your spiritual mind? It is by the Word of God and the revelation of His Word.

Why do you need to know this? Do you want to be used by God in a supernatural way? Do you want to know the ways of God? Do you want to be able to look into a situation and know what God knows about it? Would you like to look at someone and know what God knows about them? You can have accurate and clear words of knowledge and prophecy. What about the next thing God wants you to do in life? The things He wants you to do tomorrow? This is why this teaching is so important.

I have had bits and pieces of this teaching for years and have questioned God on what it all means. Where am I missing it? It is time for us to enter the new realm that God wants us to enter into in order to touch this world the way God wants us to.

1 Chronicles 28:9; "And thou, Solomon my son, know thou the God of thy father, and serve him with a perfect heart [the inner man] **and with a willing mind** [not just the natural mind only. We cannot serve God with the natural mind.]**: for the LORD searcheth all hearts, and understandeth all the imaginations of the thoughts: if thou seek him, he will be found of thee; but if thou forsake him, he will cast thee off for ever."**

God wants us to have a willing mind. Your spiritual heart has to have a willing mind. One aspect of your mind is that you have choice. You can choose or decide with both your natural mind as well as your spiritual mind. There are choices you have to make. Those choices determine the direction of your life. If you have a rotten life, it is because you have made some bad choices. A good life means some good choices. If you choose to sin, the wages of sin is death. If you chose to serve, obey, love, walk with God and do what He says you will have a good life. Your life goes the way of your choices.

Proverbs 23:7; "For as he thinketh in his heart,…"

---

[3] Ephesians 4:17-23

28

If your heart can think then it must have a mind.

Hebrews 4:12; "For the word of God is quick, and powerful, and sharper than any twoedged sword, piercing even to the dividing asunder of soul and spirit, and of the joints and marrow, and is <u>a discerner of the thoughts and intents of the heart</u>."

We have all heard the term "the mind of Christ". The mind of Christ is not in your head. It is in your heart.

Being Willing

Isaiah 1:19; "If ye be willing and obedient, ye shall eat the good of the land:"

It takes being both willing and obedient to prosper, and to eat the good of the land.

Hebrews 5:11-14; "Of whom we have many things to say, and hard to be uttered, seeing ye are dull of hearing. For when for the time ye ought to be teachers, ye have need that one teach you again which be the first principles of the oracles of God; and are become such as have need of milk, and not of strong meat. For every one that useth milk is unskilful in the word of righteousness: for he is a babe. But strong meat belongeth to them that are of full age [mature], **even those who by reason of use have their <u>senses</u> exercised to discern both good and evil."**

In the Greek senses means organs of perception, sensory receptors.

The same way there are five natural senses for your natural man that are operated by your natural mind, there are five spiritual senses for your spiritual man operated by your spiritual mind. Both of those will enable you to operate in the realm you are supposed to operate in. Your natural senses won't work in the spirit. Try to see in the spirit with your natural eyes. You will be sweating, staining and unable to see a thing in the spirit. Try to hear God with your natural ears. It will never work. Your natural sight and hearing only work in the natural.

We have something to do with being able to use those sensory receptors. If you want to see something in the natural, you have to be willing to look at it on purpose. It takes focusing on what you want to see. You have to do the same thing in the spirit realm.

Proverbs 4:20; "My son, attend to my words; incline thine ear unto my sayings."

Give attention to what is being said.

When you are talking to a child who is looking around and squirming, do you have their attention? Are they hearing you? They may give you the correct answer, but did they really hear what you said? Later on when they haven't done what you told them to do and you scold them, they will tell you they didn't hear what you said. The reason they didn't hear it is because you didn't have their attention.

Incline means to stretch toward the person who is talking to you. Get close enough to distinguish what they are really saying to you.

Proverbs 4:21; "Let them not depart from thine eyes [focus]**; keep them in the midst of thine heart. For they are life unto those that find them, and health to all their flesh. Keep thy heart with all diligence; for out of it are the issues of** [the forces, power that produces and creates] **life."**

These verses are talking about your spiritual organs of perception. The five spiritual organs of perception, your spiritual senses, are exactly the same as your natural man has. They just operate in another realm.

Hearing and Seeing

Matthew 13:13; "Therefore speak I to them in parables: because they seeing see not; and hearing they hear not, neither do they understand."

They are not hearing because they are using their natural ears and not their heart.

Matthew 13:14; "And in them is fulfilled the prophecy of Esaias, which saith, By hearing ye shall hear, and shall not understand; and seeing ye shall see, and shall not perceive:"

In the spirit realm, until I perceive and understand something I have not seen or heard. It is not that I heard a noise, but that I perceived what was being said and understood what was being revealed. That is seeing and hearing. My sensory receptors pulled it up, sent it to my spiritual brain, the light bulb turned on and I got it. My spiritual brain processed it and came up with the right conclusion.

Matthew 13:15; "For this people's heart is waxed gross [hard], and their ears are dull of hearing [got tired of hearing it], and their eyes they have closed; lest at any time they should see with their eyes, and hear with their ears, and should understand with their heart, and should be converted, and I should heal them."

These verses are about a person's will. Spiritually, you can hear if you want to hear. Spiritually, you can see if you want to see, but you are going to have to do it on purpose. You are going to give God some time. You can't run into your prayer closet, pray hard and fast, jump up and run out not giving God time to talk to you, to reveal and show you something. Corporate prayer should be more intercessory and directive. Devotional prayer should be more listening. Pray in tongues then listen, sense and feel. You will be surprised what you get.

Verse 15 says that if you would see and hear, you would understand and be healed. When you start picking things up with your

31

spiritual senses, you will start receiving manifestations of God. When your spiritual senses start operating, you are in a receiving mode.

Now I want you to see that being in the spirit has very little to do with your natural circumstances.

Revelation 1:9; "I John, who also am your brother, and companion in tribulation, and in the kingdom and patience of Jesus Christ, was in the isle that is called Patmos, for the word of God, and for the testimony of Jesus Christ."

John is letting us know he is going through tribulation, trouble. They had tried to kill him by boiling him in oil and it didn't work. Now they have put him on a desert island to die. No food or drinking water, no shelter, extreme temperatures during the day and night. In the midst of this terrible discomfort, John says something interesting.

Revelation 1:10; "I was in the Spirit on the Lord's day, and heard behind me a great voice, as of a trumpet,"

We are housed in flesh, but it has nothing to do with the spirit. You can be going through all sorts of problems and have peace in your life. In the spirit realm you can be having an awesome time with God and it will bring you out of the trouble you are in.

Romans 8:9; "But ye are not in the flesh, <u>but in the Spirit, if so be that the Spirit of God dwell in you...</u>"

Dwell in this verse means to dominate, to control you. You are controlled by the Spirit of God and have your mind on the things of the spirit. <u>When you and I have our minds on the things of the spirit, we are in the spirit.</u>

What does it mean to be in the Spirit? It is to have your spiritual mind stayed on Him. You are thinking, meditating on the Lord.

Where is your focus? That will determine whether you are in the flesh or the spirit.

John heard. Why did he hear? It was because he was focusing, looking into the realm of the spirit. His mind was on spiritual things, therefore he could hear.

Some people will complain because they never hear God and don't know what the problem is. They have been focusing on the wrong thing, most of the time it is television.

Revelation 1:12; "And I turned to see the voice that spake with me. And being turned, I saw seven golden candlesticks;"

John turned to see. Turned means to focus toward the things of God. It is almost connected to the word repent. Turn in another direction. Quit going the way of the flesh and wrapping your life around everything here on the earth. The way we are in the physical will not last forever. It will end. We will pass on and go to either heaven or hell.

If you learn to live by the things of the spirit, you will walk in victory even in the natural realm. The world is doing the opposite and they are in trouble. It isn't working for them.

God wants us to live according to the spirit, but we can't unless we are operating in the spirit because we are focusing on the things of the spirit. We can never operate in the spirit until we focus on the things of the spirit. It takes our spiritual senses to be able to do it.

If you are a child of God, where is the Holy Spirit? He is in you. So where is He going to speak to you? It will be on the inside of you. If He speaks to the inside of you, it will literally be thought to thought. You will know things you didn't know. It is still a voice, but it is processed by your spiritual mind.

Have you ever known something and didn't know how you knew it? Maybe it was about a person, place or thing. Or you meet somebody and they say one thing while you know something else they never said. That was the Holy Spirit within you and your spiritual receptors were picking it up. Your spiritual mind was active otherwise you couldn't know. How do you know something? It is because you have a mind. It is a spiritual mind, the mind of Christ.

Feeling

Hebrews 4:15; "For we have not an high priest which cannot be touched with the feeling of our infirmities [anything that hurts us]**; but was in all points tempted like as we are, yet without sin."**

Feeling in the Greek is *sumpatheo (soom-path-eh'-o)*. It means sympathy pains. One person called it fellow feelings – feeling someone else's pain whether it is emotional, physically or a loss.

When your sense of spiritual feeling is operating at a high level and those sensory receptors are at work and you are aware of it in your spiritual mind, then the gifts of healings begin to work. You will begin feeling things in your own body. There may be pain in your right knee and you know there is nothing wrong with it. Maybe you walk past somebody and a deep sadness comes over you. You know that you are not sad. A thought of suicide may come when you are walking past someone.

In Russia one time the hearing in my one ear began to go out and then open up with a big pop. I knew there was nothing wrong with my ear so I called out for someone with a deaf ear. Their ear opened up. It was the Holy Spirit letting me know.

These are sympathetic pains in your spirit man and your receptors are picking them up.

Acts 17:27; "That they should seek the Lord, if haply they might feel after him, and find him, though he be not far from every one of us:"

In the natural, your natural feelings can hinder your faith. In the spirit it is totally different. Your spiritual feelings aid your faith. This is why we walk by faith and not by sight.

You can get up one day and in the natural things are bad, but inside you have an inner feeling that it will be the greatest days you ever had. It is not a natural feeling, but a supernatural one that you are picking up and feeling. What does that do to your faith? It aids it.

Remember the woman with the issue of blood who touched the hem of Jesus' garment? The Bible tells us that Jesus felt virtue leave His body. The virtue was spiritual, not natural. What He felt was something spiritual. Have you ever laid hands on the sick and had something come up out of you and into that person? What you felt was a power. Was that real? A physical sensation? No, although it might have been so strong you thought it was physical. While it affected the natural, it was actually a spiritual sensation that could be felt first and foremost by the spirit, your spiritual man.

Taste

Psalms 34:8; "O taste and see that the LORD is good: blessed is the man that trusteth in him."

We know that the Lord is spiritual. How are you going to taste Him - with your natural taste buds? You cannot. Taste Him with your spiritual taste buds.

To taste something you generally have to do it on purpose. Someone is eating a blueberry cobbler with ice cream on top. They are just going on about how good it tastes and offer you a bite. You have to open your mouth on purpose to receive it. Once you have it, you have to move it around on your tongue to taste it. It is the same way in the spirit. You have to do it on purpose. Partake of the Lord and savor the flavor of God and His Word. Take time to enjoy it.

Can you see where your mind and your decision process are involved? A lot of people are not experiencing God at all because there is no decision. They are expecting it to come on them like something dropping out of a tree on to their head, but it has to be on purpose by a spiritual decision using your spiritual mind.

Psalms 119:103; "How sweet are thy words unto my taste! yea, sweeter than honey to my mouth!"

What mouth is being talked about? It is the spiritual mouth.

I have heard it said that we are living below our privileges in God. I believe it. We are in a season now where if we are going to make it then we need to be operating in a another realm.

Do you want to make it financially no matter what happens with the stock market or with the economy? You can do it by operating from the spirit into the natural. Adam and Eve operated from spirit, soul and then body. When they sinned, the order was reversed and became body, soul and spirit. If you will develop the spirit realm and walk in the spirit you will find that it will radically affect and empower the natural realm. You will prosper, be blessed and walk in health. You will have the glory, the mind, the thoughts, the fullness, the success and the power of God.

Smelling

When you are moving in the spirit, you have a nice fragrance.

Psalms 45:8; "All thy garments smell of myrrh, and aloes, and cassia, out of the ivory palaces, whereby they have made thee glad."

The psalmist is talking about the garments of our Lord.

God has a wonderful aroma about Him. Have you ever been in a service and you began to smell flowers or perfume?

Song of Solomon 2:1; "I am the rose of Sharon, and the lily of the valleys."

This is speaking of our Lord. If He is the rose of Sharon and the lily of the valley, will we smell roses and lilies in a meeting when His presence is strong? Everyone could smell them if they understood what it takes to smell. You have to smell on purpose by sniffing in order to get the aroma into your nose. You have to want to smell something.

In Mark 9:25 Jesus was casting out demons and He called them foul spirits. Demons stink. Dead spirits that are cut off from the life of God, they are decaying and reek of bad odor.

A poverty spirit has an odor. It smells like old musty clothes that have been down in a cellar. A spirit of insanity smells like urine. Cancer has a unique scent that is not natural. Homosexual spirits have a horrible smell. I can smell alcohol and drugs on people who are bound by them. Even if they haven't been drinking at the time, I can smell alcohol from a distance.

Hebrews 5:14; "But strong meat belongeth to them that are of full age, even those who by reason of use have their senses exercised to discern both good and evil."

All of these spiritual senses are available so that we can discern both good and evil. Discern means judicial estimation, to separate thoroughly, to decide correctly, to distinguish between that which is holy and of God and that which is not.[4]

---

[4] More can be found on the five spiritual senses in our School of the Prophets course.

Receive the Word of God

We are going to be talking about coming to the place where your spiritual mind becomes highly developed so that you can receive the thoughts of God.

Isaiah 55:8-9; "For my thoughts are not your thoughts, neither are your ways my ways, saith the LORD. For as the heavens are higher than the earth, so are my ways higher than your ways, and my thoughts than your thoughts."

When we read these verses out of context it sounds like there is no way we can think like God thinks or know His ways. To keep it in context read verse 7.

Isaiah 55:7; "Let the wicked forsake his way, and the unrighteous man his thoughts: and let him return unto the LORD, and he will have mercy upon him; and to our God, for he will abundantly pardon."

We are to forsake our way of thinking and doing. Then God says His ways are higher and that man has not known them. It is true that the natural mind cannot take on the thoughts of God. Your natural mind can only think natural thoughts, but you have a spirit man on the inside of you that has a mind. If that spiritual mind is renewed to the Word of God, it can think the thoughts of God and can know the ways of the Lord. That's what God desires. If you read these verses in context you will see that is what God is talking about. He wants you to know His thoughts. He wants you to know His ways. Otherwise, how are you going to obey and follow

Him? How are we going to do His will? We have to know His thoughts and His ways.

In the last chapter we talked about your natural mind enabling your five senses to operate. It is the same way with your spiritual mind. Your spiritual mind enables your five spiritual senses to operate.

Your eyes, nose, ears, mouth and skin are sensory receptors that receive information and stimuli from the environment and turn it into electrical impulses. These impulses are sent to our brain. Your brain is the one that sees, hears, smells, tastes and touches. In the natural realm our mind is very important.

In the spirit realm it is the same way. We must develop our spiritual minds in order to fully develop our spiritual senses so we can hear God, see into the spirit, feel His presence better, smell His fragrance and taste and see that the Lord is good. The more you develop your spiritual mind, the stronger those spiritual senses become.

I want to give you five ways that we are to develop our spiritual mind so that our spiritual senses will become very strong and we will be able to operate with the mind of Christ. We will be able to receive His thoughts and know His ways in every situation of our life. We will never be in darkness or never be in a place where we don't know what to do. This is important to the body of Christ. If we ever needed this message, we need it now.

Being Taught

Hebrews 5:12; "For when for the time ye ought to be teachers, ye have need that one teach you again which be the first principles of the oracles of God; and are become such as have need of milk, and not of strong meat."

The very first point in developing the mind of Christ is that we must be taught the Word of God by the fivefold ministry. Verse 12 says very plainly that being taught the Word of God is the first principle of becoming an oracle.

I want to talk about an oracle for a little.

1 Kings 6:19; "And the oracle he prepared in the house within, to set there the ark of the covenant of the LORD."

This verse is talking about Solomon building the temple. The Word says that we are the temple of the Holy Ghost. The Spirit of God dwells within us. When you look at Solomon's temple and the tabernacle that was in the wilderness there were three parts to them just as there are three parts to us. We have a body, soul and spirit. The inner part, called the Holy of Holies, is a type and shadow of our spirit. That is where the Ark of the Covenant was and from where God would speak and commune with the people.

John 8:31-32; "Then said Jesus to those Jews which believed on him, If ye continue in my word, then are ye my disciples indeed; And ye shall know the truth, and the truth shall make you free."

A disciple is a disciplined learner and disciplined follower. It is important to understand that when people come to Christ they become converts first. Then they must become disciples and a disciple in the Word of God. Disciple means disciplined to come to the house of God and be taught the Word of God. Some people stay converts all their lives and never get to discipleship. Once you hit discipleship you can come into becoming sons of God. According to 1 John the next step is becoming spiritual mothers and fathers in the faith. That is the progression, but if you never become a disciple you will never go any further in God.

2 Corinthians 3:2-3; "Ye are our epistle written in our hearts, known and read of all men: Forasmuch as ye are manifestly declared to be the epistle of Christ ministered by us, written not with ink, but with

the Spirit of the living God; not in tables of stone, but in fleshy tables of the heart."

God wants us to become the Word of God, but you can't do that until you are discipled into the Word of God. You have to be taught the Word of God to become an oracle. An oracle means a mouth piece of the Word, the place where God speaks. He wants us to become His Word to the world, a living epistle. A living epistle is the living Word of God. Oracle literally comes from the same word we get logos from. The oracle is the living word.

The only Bible that most people will ever read is you and me. but we cannot become that until we are taught the Word. When do we stop being taught the Word? Never. It is an ongoing process until we leave this world. There is always more. If you ever stop growing spiritually you digress and back slide.

2 Corinthians 4:16; "For which cause we faint not; but though our outward man perish, yet the inward man is <u>renewed</u> day by day."

How do you renew the inner man?

Romans 12:1-2; "I beseech you therefore, brethren, by the mercies of God, that ye present your bodies a living sacrifice, holy, acceptable unto God, which is your reasonable service. And be not conformed to this world: but be ye transformed by the renewing of your mind, that ye may prove what is that good, and acceptable, and perfect, will of God."

The mind mentioned in these verses is the inner man that is being renewed after the knowledge of Christ. Your natural mind deals with natural thoughts and cannot be renewed. It is what it is. Thank God that our natural mind helps us operate in the natural. Use it as a tool to operate in the natural, but don't let it rule you. Your spirit man should be ruling over your natural man telling your natural mind what to think. When your natural mind wants to think the wrong thing, you correct it. When your natural man wants to sin, you tell it you are not going to do that. It takes a strong inner man to override the outer man.

Romans 8:13; "For if ye live after the flesh, ye shall die: but if ye through the Spirit do mortify the deeds of the body, ye shall live."

How do you overcome the lusts of the flesh? It is by the power of the Spirit of God within your inner man. Build up the inner man and it will override the outer man and bring him into check.

Ephesians 4:22-23; "That ye put off concerning the former conversation the old man, which is corrupt according to the deceitful lusts; And be renewed in the spirit of your mind;"

Be renewed in your spirit man by the Word of God. Feed the Word into your spiritual mind because it can handle revelation. Your natural mind cannot.

Hebrews 4:12; "For the word of God is quick, and powerful, and sharper than any two edged sword, piercing even to the dividing asunder of soul and spirit, and of the joints and marrow, and is a discerner of the <u>thoughts and intents of the heart</u>."

The Word of God is a discerner of the thoughts of the heart. It means that your heart can think. It has a mind. Remember, we are talking about your inner man, your spirit man.

We must have the Word of God fed into the mind of our spirit because it will divide the thoughts that are not of God from those which are of God so that you can rightly judge thoughts when they come. You won't then say every thought that comes is from God. It is only by knowing the Word of God and having enough Word inside of you that can you know the difference. Only the Word can discern it.

Colossians 2:7; "Rooted and built up in him, and stablished in the faith, <u>as ye have been taught</u>, abounding therein with thanksgiving."

We will be rooted and built up in the spirit because we have been taught the Word of God.

Eat Strong Meat

Secondly we need to eat strong meat.

Hebrews 5:12 tells us that we need to be eating strong meat. Strong in the Greek means to eat meat that is steadfast, solid. We need to eat strong meat, meaning that which brings nourishment or strength. We need good, solid, stable teaching of the Word. We need to be taught the Word that we actually need to chew on. It is not easily understood at the time and must be chewed on for a little while. In other words, it may be something you have not heard before, maybe some fresh revelation. If it is, that is okay as long as there is enough scripture to substantiate it. In the mouth of two or three witnesses shall every word be established.[5] We need a volume of scripture to know that we are on the right track. The scripture should also be in context.

Don't submit yourself to just anybody who is teaching the Word. Know them that labor among you. Connect to people who are connected to people.

2 Timothy 2:15; "Study to shew thyself approved unto God, a workman that needeth not to be ashamed, rightly dividing the word of truth."

If you don't study the Word, you can wrongly divide it. If you have not been taught the Word, you can wrongly divide it. Just reading the Word is not enough. It is the start of study, but it is not enough. You have to go beyond just reading the Word. You have to come to the house of God and be taught the Word or you will come up with some doctrine that is not God.

In John 6:53 Jesus was talking to the people who were following Him in a language they didn't understand. He didn't try to make His message understandable to everyone. In fact, He said that the reason He spoke to the people in parables was so they couldn't understand it. He complicated it so only the ones who were going to become disciples would

---

[5] 2 Corinthians 13:1

43

follow Him. Jesus would explain it to those who followed Him because He didn't want to cast His pearls before a swine mentality. That is wisdom.

Don't tell the world all the awesome things Jesus is doing for you by the spirit in detail. They can't handle it. You can tell them that He has changed your life and is the only way to heaven. You can also tell them He has healed you. Leave it at that. Don't give them strong doctrine, the deep things the Holy Spirit has given you. They can't and aren't supposed to handle it until they come and receive all that God has, pressing in to become disciples.

I can show you in scripture where the children of Israel would only go just so far up the mount and stop. The seventy elders, with Moses and Joshua, went a little farther up the mountain. Joshua and Moses went a little higher. Then Moses went the rest of the way up by himself. The farther you go with God, the fewer the people who go with you.

Jesus only truly had twelve disciples. The seventy took off when He started giving them deep stuff. The crowd also left. Jesus looked at the twelve and asked if they were going to leave Him also.

John 6:68; "Then Simon Peter answered him, Lord, to whom shall we go? thou hast the words of eternal life."

Peter came through with a revelation.

In other words, the disciples are the only ones who can handle the deep revelation of the Word. The average Christian can't and won't even stay for it. They will leave.

In one church the youth pastor came up to me and said he never really liked me. I already knew that. He would come in late, sit in the back and leave early. He didn't want to hear about the prophetic or miracles, feeling there was no need for them. Then he found out he was dying from an incurable blood disease.

This man picked me up to go out and eat. While we were waiting for our table, he began to cry saying he had to have me because he was dying. He wanted to hear about the miracles I had seen. So, for two hours I talked about the miracles. I told of a dead baby being raised up, ear drums being created, teeth filled, the eyeball that God created for a boy who had none and on and on. At the end of each story, he would ask for another one. When he took me back to my hotel room he asked me to pray over him. I rebuked the blood disease, commanded it to leave and spoke healing into his body.

The next day as I was ministering I heard the first name of a doctor. I happened to be standing near this man when I said I saw the first name of a doctor and he was giving somebody a good report on a Monday or a Tuesday morning. He jumped up and ran out of the meeting. I wondered if I had offended him.

The building we were meeting in was a two story building. This man did not know the first name of his doctor so he had gone upstairs to the office and grabbed a phone book. After a few minutes, he came running back to the service calling out that the name was the first name of his doctor and he was scheduled to go back for another blood test. I said that he was going to get a different report this time and he answered he had known it when I prayed for him the day before.

He called me after I had left and returned home. When he went in to see the doctor they took another blood test. The doctor sat down with him and said it was the strangest thing. It was as if the antibodies in his body had become supercharged and had eaten up all the disease. He didn't have the disease anymore. After telling the doctor that he knew it, the doctor wanted to know how. He told the doctor that a man of God had said the first name of the doctor and that he was going to be giving the man a good report. The doctor said it was his first name and he had given a good report.

God wants us to receive what He has for us. We need to become disciples and love the revelation of the Word. We also need to love the fivefold ministry even if it doesn't seem to be our cup of tea at the moment. You may prefer pastoral preaching, but you need to love the evangelist as well. You need to love what the prophet does when he preaches and teaches. You need to love what the apostle does when he comes with divine order and sets order.

Develop a taste for what the fivefold ministry does when they teach and preach the Word. Without it you will never develop into who God wants you to be.

Jesus says some very unusual things in John 6:53.

John 6:53; "Then Jesus said unto them, Verily, verily, I say unto you, Except ye eat the flesh of the Son of man, and drink his blood, ye have no life in you."

At the time Jesus said this there was a cult living by the Dead Sea who were into cannibalism. Jesus knew all of that and still said we needed to eat His flesh and drink His blood. He knew He was going to shake people who weren't serious about Him. These were the people who came for the loaves and fishes, for what they could get instead of what they could give to the Lord. They came to get their healing, their prosperity, their free meal. Did they think about serving God? Not really.

John 6:55-59; "For my flesh is meat indeed, and my blood is drink indeed. He that eateth my flesh, and drinketh my blood, dwelleth in me, and I in him. As the living Father hath sent me, and I live by the Father: so he that eateth me, even he shall live by me. This is that bread which came down from heaven: not as your fathers did eat manna, and are dead: he that eateth of this bread shall live for ever. These things said he in the synagogue, as he taught in Capernaum."

Some do not understand what Jesus was saying in these verses. When He said eat of His flesh, He was saying we must eat of His Word. He is the living Word.

John 1:14; "And the Word was made flesh..."

When you eat of the revelation of the Word, you are eating of Jesus. You are taking Him into your spirit and He said you would have life in you.

He also said that we must drink of His blood. When I studied blood, I found that the life of the flesh is in the blood. Life means the spirit. So when you drink of His Spirit you are drinking of His blood.

Eat of the revelation of His Word and drink in of His Spirit. If you will do that, you will have life in you.

If you want to think His thoughts, you have to eat of the meat.

There is one more thing about meat that I want you to see.

Jesus had gone to Samaria. He knew by the mind of the Spirit that He needed to be in Samaria at a well at noon because there would be a woman there who needed Him. If you and I develop our spiritual minds, we can handle the same kind of thoughts.

Let me give you an example of this. A close friend of mine has a ministry of street witnessing. I told him I would like to go with him sometime because I had done it in the early days of my ministry. At one church I had done street witnessing for three months. I wanted to see how he did it.

He told me to meet him one Saturday morning about nine o'clock. When we meet, he told me that in about five to ten minutes we had to leave to pick up a lady who was in front of a grocery store with all of her groceries. She had ice cream in a bag and was afraid would melt. Her son was supposed to pick her up, but he wouldn't be coming because he was doing something else. I thought he had gotten a phone call from this lady. What I didn't know was he had spent two hours in prayer before I arrived and knew these things by the spirit.

We drove to the grocery store and there was a woman sitting outside with bags of groceries. We stopped and he asked her if he could help. She said that her son was supposed to be there to pick her up. That was exactly what he had said to me before we arrived. He told her we were ministers and would help her out by taking her home. She answered that we might as well so the ice cream didn't melt. We took her home, unloaded her groceries and he gave her a couple of tracts. Then he told her that he had been praying, had seen her face and saw her sitting on the curb waiting for her son. With that he had also known exactly what time we needed to come and pick her up. She asked how he knew all of that and he began to minister to her.

God wants us to hit that realm of glory thoughts. God knew she would be there with groceries, including ice cream. He knew that her son would not show up and she would be sitting on the curb at nine o'clock in the morning. Do you want to operate by your spiritual mind? If you develop it, you can. That is where the body of Christ needs to be. With the fivefold ministering to you and you becoming a student of the Word of God, you can do that.

Jesus sent His disciples to town to get something to eat, to get meat for Him. They came back with the meal and look at what He said to them.

John 4:32; "But he said unto them, I have meat to eat that ye know not of."

The disciples were a little upset, wondering if someone had brought Him something to eat. They had gone to town and shopped for the food He wanted. If they had known He would get something to eat, they could have stayed at the well with Him.

Jesus explained what He meant.

John 4:34; "Jesus saith unto them, My meat is to do the will of him that sent me, and to finish his work."

Not only is meat the deep revelation of Jesus and His Word, it is also to reach out and help somebody else, to love somebody, to minister to somebody. I am looking for the day the body of Christ realizes that not only are we supposed to be eating, but we are also supposed to be feeding somebody else.

Here is the third point on how to develop the mind of Christ.

Being of Full Age

Hebrews 5:14; "But strong meat belongeth to them that are of <u>full age</u>, even those who by reason of use have their senses exercised to discern both good and evil."

Full age means maturity. Maturity doesn't just come by years in the spirit realm. Maturity comes with how much you press into God with intensity. I know young people who have so pressed into God for two or three years that they are more mature than some who have been saved for fifty years. Going to church but not praying or reading the Word of God is not maturity. I want to see maturity that comes from people who have spent time with God in prayer and the Word on a regular basis.

How do we come into full maturity?

Let me show what the Word says about maturity connected to the fivefold ministry. If we don't have a fivefold ministry we still won't come to maturity.

Ephesians 4:11-12; "And he gave some, apostles; and some, prophets; and some, evangelists; and some, pastors and teachers; For the perfecting [equipping] of the saints, for the work of the ministry, for the edifying of the body of Christ:"

The saints are the one who are supposed to be doing the work of the ministry and the edifying of the body of Christ.

Ephesians 4:13-16; "Till we all come in the unity of the faith, and of the knowledge of the Son of God, unto a <u>perfect</u> [mature] <u>man</u>, unto the measure of the stature of the fulness of Christ: That we henceforth be no more children, tossed to and fro, and carried about with every wind of doctrine, by the sleight of men, and cunning craftiness, whereby they lie in wait to deceive; But speaking the truth in love,

49

may <u>grow up</u> into him in all things, which is the head, even Christ: From whom the whole body fitly joined together and compacted by that which every joint supplieth, according to the effectual working in the measure of every part, maketh increase of the body unto the edifying of itself in love."

These verses tell us that the fivefold ministry is supposed to help the body come to maturity. That means without the fivefold the church won't come to full maturity. We must be ministered to by the fivefold ministry.

By Reason of Use

Hebrews 5:14; "But strong meat belongeth to them that are of full age, even those who by reason of use have their senses exercised to discern both good and evil."

Reason of use means that you need to be a doer of the Word of God. It is not enough to be taught it; you need to be doing it. So, have a heart to implement what you have been taught. If you are not a doer of the Word, your spiritual mind will not be developed.

James 1:22; "But be ye doers of the word, and not hearers only, deceiving your own selves."

When you have a mind that says you know what is right, but you are not doing it then you are deceived. You don't know it. When you really get the Word of God in your spiritual mind, then revelation brings motivation. If you think that just knowing it from your head is going to be enough, you have been deceived and many Christians are deceived. When you are doing something that you have a revelation of, now you are on the right track. Without a heart revelation of something, you have no motivation to do anything. Get a true revelation about giving and you will be giving. Get a true revelation about healing and you will be receiving healing. Get a true revelation about the gifts of the spirit and you will start operating in it. Get a revelation about prayer and you will be praying. I can always tell when someone has a revelation or just natural head knowledge. All I need to do is watch them.

50

James 1:23-24; "For if any be a hearer of the word, and not a doer, he is like unto a man beholding his natural face in a glass: For he beholdeth himself, and goeth his way, and straightway forgetteth what manner of man he was."

In other words, without doing God's Word you don't know who you are.

James 1:25; "But whoso looketh into the perfect law of liberty [theWord of God], and continueth therein, he being not a forgetful hearer, but a doer of the work, this man shall be blessed in his deed."

What is this man doing? He is doing the Word. Get a revelation of the Word and do it so you can be blessed. We are blessed by doing the Word, not just having a head knowledge of it. You need to get heart knowledge in your spiritual mind and the motivation will be there to do it. Get it on the inside of you and you will do it.

This verse talks about use, practice and habit. Did you know that if you pray for twenty-one consecutive days you will be in the prayer habit? The same is true of Bible reading and study. Just survive twenty-one days and you will have the motivation. It will become a habit and you will keep on doing it. As you continue a habit, it becomes a life style. A life style becomes a nature and a nature becomes a destiny.

Exercise Your Senses

Hebrews 5:14; "But strong meat belongeth to them that are of full age, even those who by reason of use have their senses exercised to discern both good and evil."

Exercised means to take your senses and begin to use them.

Jude 1:20; "But ye, beloved, building up yourselves on your most holy faith, praying in the Holy Ghost,"

When you pray in the Spirit you begin to exercise your spirit man.

51

The more you use your spiritual senses, the stronger they get and the more accurate they become.

Habakkuk 2:1; "I will stand upon my watch, and set me upon the tower, and will watch to see what he will say unto me, and what I shall answer when I am reproved."

"Stand upon the watch" refers to towering or getting into prayer. We need to get into prayer and listen to God.

"I will watch to see what He will say to me". This means I will get into prayer, ask some specific questions of the Holy Spirit, pray softly in tongues and listen, look, taste, smell and feel. I will get a pad of paper and start writing down impressions, little things that come to me.

Have you ever heard of the Urim and Thummin? These were two stones that were put in a little bag behind the breastplate of the high priest. He would ask a question of God and pull out the stones. One stone meant illumination. The other stone basically meant judgment or discerning. When the question was asked one stone would light up and meant yes.

A question might be *"Should we go to war?"* The high priest would pull out the stones and look at them. One would light up and the answer would be yes.

The physical stones can no longer be found, but they are in our spirit. Lights (revelation) and discernment are now in us. Most of us have experienced them in our lives, but we get busy operating by our head instead of our heart and do no listen to what we are hearing inside. We need to develop the mind of Christ so we can know what He knows, know His ways and know the flowing thoughts of God.

I have learned that with every situation I start back at ground zero because every situation is different. Every service is different. I can't minister one night the way I did in a previous service. I can handle that change though because I move by the Spirit. Now, some things will stay constant.

The constant is that I am going to have introspection, by seeking and searching out the leadership of the Lord with my inner senses. I am going to be looking with the eyes of my heart and listening with the ears of my heart. I will be feeling with my spirit so I can know what I cannot know. I will watch for certain thoughts that are flowing, not coming from my head but from my spirit. In other words, if I just know something I will flow with it. It can be a knowing something about somebody that I have no knowledge of. That being the case, I will check it out because it is probably from the Lord.

If I am fearful, I will never check it out. There is always a risk to the natural when operating in the spirit. I could have heard wrong or missed something. Maybe it was not for that time but for a future one.

Kim Clement has said there are three types of people. There are the care takers who take too much care when it comes to stepping out and doing what God says. They play it safe by staying in the boat when God says to step out. Then there are the undertakers. This group waits until someone else messes up and then help bury the situation. The last group is the risk takers who listen to the voice of God and step out of the boat when God says come. Which group do you fit it into? Everyone falls into one of these three groups.

There have been times when I have hopped back and forth between the three, but I want to live my life as a risk taker and not just for the sake of taking a risk. I want to hear His voice and step out of the boat. Don't get out of the boat if you have not heard the Lord say to come. If you are not getting an impression, don't check it out. "*I am not hearing or seeing anything.*" Then don't do anything.

I learned a long time ago that only that which is of God produces. If God is not saying it I can't make it happen.

Sometimes we are not sensitive and miss the fact that He was saying something to us. When He is saying something it may be a flowing thought or a flash vision where you see a little something. There is a way to handle those impressions if you are gentle with people. Ask a question.

53

Tell what you saw and if they say it is not for them, then ask if it may be for a family member or someone else they know.

In one instance I was sitting in a restaurant and had thoughts of suicide when the waiter came to our table. I asked if anyone he knew was having those thoughts. He broke down crying and asking how I knew. I told him that I didn't know, but God did and loved Him. That is why God told me. I prayed for him and encouraged him in the Lord.

If you want to win people to Christ, you have to get rid of the religious way of thinking and doing and just be real with them. Don't use the Christian language, like "*Are you saved, sanctified and delivered?*" What does that mean to people who don't know the Lord? Be real with people. This is a part of flowing. This is how Jesus ministered to the unsaved and to those needing ministry. This is how, we too, will build the Kingdom.

Made in the USA
Columbia, SC
21 April 2021